T0208266

Make Leadership
COUNT

DR. ANTHONY J. PERKINS

authorHOUSE®

AuthorHouse™
1663 Liberty Drive
Bloomington, IN 47403
www.authorhouse.com
Phone: 1 (800) 839-8640

Published by AuthorHouse 08/13/2019

ISBN: 978-1-7283-1939-1 (sc)
ISBN: 978-1-7283-1938-4 (e)

Print information available on the last page.

This book is printed on acid-free paper.

This book is dedicated to God, my daughter, and my dad.
God, I thank you for my journey.
Talaya, I am crazy about you. You are next.
Dad, thank you for all of the life lessons.

Contents

Introduction

This book has been written for novice leaders. It will help you understand five core leadership traits that, if practiced to mastery, will build your leadership capacity and help you become a respected leader. However, a leader at any level can utilize the five core leadership traits to advance their leadership.

Leadership is a defining moment and a blessing that should be taken very seriously. Imagine waking up every morning to lead an organization, to motivate or inspire team members, and to work on goals that will lead to great accomplishments. This is the excitement you want in leadership. The enjoyment of using your influence to build up people and the organization.

There are only two reasons you should be a leader. The first is that it is a calling. A higher power has called you to inspire, transform, and **fight the good fight**. The second is that you have an A-plus passion to lead. This is it! Much too often there are people who have great talents but are not true leaders. They would be great followers. If they were honest with themselves, they would admit it and move into the right seat on the team bus. Everyone cannot be a leader.

This may be a current or a past memory—when you were young, there was that bus driver who encouraged you in the morning, there was that cafeteria lady who motivated you, there was that janitor who always said positive words to you, there was that vice principal who always pumped you up by telling you—you can do anything, and there was that teacher who pushed your potential to a higher level. Inspiring others is a big part of leadership. It is now your turn to stimulate and shape teammates.

I want to share a short story with you that correlates well with leadership: Chapter 1: I was walking down the street. There was a hole in the street, and I fell in the hole. It was not my fault. It took me a long time to get out of the hole. Chapter 2: I was walking down the street. There was a hole in the street, and I fell in the hole. It was my fault. It took me a long time to get out of the hole. Chapter 3: I was walking down the street. There was a hole in the street, and I walked around the hole. Chapter 4: I chose to walk down a different street.

Question: Why is it that many leaders never get to chapter 4, where they finally learn how to utilize their leadership knowledge, skills, and savvy to **critically think through situations** in order to reach a great decision or end result?

Let's take a journey to learn about five core leadership traits that will assist leaders in reaching their chapter 4. The five core leadership traits are…having **C**ourage, thinking **O**utside the box, practicing H**U**mility, being a **N**ipper, and **T**eaching others. If you are ready, let's make leadership COUNT!

Courage

Jim Valvano

The late great Jim Valvano, a.k.a. Jimmy V, was the North Carolina State head men's basketball coach from 1980–1990. His North Carolina State Wolfpack were in the Atlantic Coast Conference (ACC) league with bigger and more well-known universities like the University of North Carolina—which, at the time, had the great Michael Jordan; the University of Virginia, with the seven-foot center Ralph Sampson; and Duke University, with legendary Coach K and his always competitive teams.

Jimmy V arrived at the first North Carolina State basketball practice and announced to his team that they were going to win the national championship. All the players looked around with confusion but went along with it. Coach Valvano preached this point—"We are going to win the national championship"—during every practice. He added an exercise to each practice: his team rehearsed cutting down the basketball net as if they had just won a championship.

What was he doing? He was being a courageous leader and **painting a vision** for his team. He was having the team marinate in his winning words with the goal of shifting their mind-sets from *me* to *we*.

Year one, his team did not even make the National Collegiate Athletic Association (NCAA) tournament. The NCAA tournament is the tournament that teams need to qualify for in order to win the national championship. Each team, once they qualify for the NCAA tournament, must win six games in a row to become the national champions.

Year two, Coach Valvano's team qualified for the NCAA tournament but lost in the first round. Year three, Coach Valvano's team qualified for the NCAA tournament but lost in the second round. Year four, Coach Valvano's team's record was not good, and the only method to qualify for the NCAA tournament was to win the ACC tournament.

Now remember, the teams in the ACC were powerhouses such as Duke University with Coach K, the University of North Carolina with Michael Jordan, and the University of Virginia with the powerful Ralph Sampson. This was a tall order to win all of their games against such talent. Guess what? They did manage to **beat the odds** and squeak out last-minute victories to become the ACC champions. This automatically qualified them for the NCAA tournament.

That was miracle one. Now the Wolfpack had to win six games in a row to become the national champions, which had been the goal all along. This was another monumental task. Out of the five tournament games they played leading up to the championship game, only one game was not close.

The other four games were last-second victories. The team's nickname was the Cardiac Kids, due to their last-second heroics.

Their sixth and final game, the NCAA championship, also came down to the last seconds. A shot was forced from three-point range but was short; another NC State player intercepted the basketball in the air at the rim to slam-dunk it a second before the clock expired at zero. North Carolina State won the NCAA National Championship in 1983.

Coach Valvano instilled in his players from the first practice that they were going to win the national championship, and they did. He had not recruited those players and did not even know them well at that point. **Courageous leaders take risks**, stick their necks out, inspire, motivate, and teach as they continue through their journey. Remember, the team's journey was not easy; they lost many games and were behind many times only to triumph as the victors. Through their journey there were many doubts and frustrations, but they stayed the course and believed they would reach their goal.

Courageous leadership is needed in organizations. Leadership is *not* about being static, comfortable, and lacking movement. It is all about moving your team forward, taking risks, and following a strategic plan through the ups and downs. If you are going to sit in the leadership chair, you must take risks. **Go out on a limb**, as that is where the fruit grows.

To get anything of great value,
you have to sacrifice.

Former President Barack Obama

When you review the tasks former president Barack Obama had on his plate as president, it is impressive and surpasses most presidents' lists of tasks and accomplishments. He inherited two wars, the mortgage crisis, and the automobile bailout; passed the Affordable Care Act; ordered the killing of two dictators; worked hard at handling cultural tensions between police and black citizens due to many police shootings of black men in the United States; tried to resolve random shootings in schools across the United States (but congress would not approve gun-control measures); and came up with a resolution that did not result in additional loss of lives in regard to Syria and its chemical use.

If you take all of these concerns and add the fact that the Republican Party refused to work with him during his administration, I am surprised former president Obama did not snap and jump off a bridge. He had to be very frustrated. What I appreciate about him is that he kept a courageous and positive attitude. Former first lady Michelle Obama stated, "When they go low, we go high." These motivational words from his wife most likely helped former president Obama to stay the course and **do the right things**.

There are two acts former president Obama accomplished during his presidency that were very courageous. The first act was Obamacare, also known as the Affordable Care Act. Presidents in this country have been trying to pass some form of universal health care for one hundred years without success.

Other countries offer universal health care to their citizens, and their health care systems are working out fine.

For some reason when a United States president would pursue universal health care, it became damaging to his administration, and he would be told it could hurt his chances for reelection. Because of this, former presidents stopped their quest and conformed to the status quo thinking—meaning, first you get along, and then you go along. This is *not* leadership. It is being a puppet—a yes-man. It means doing what your constituents want in order to get reelected. True leadership is about doing what is right regardless of the consequences. Dr. Martin Luther King Jr. and former president John F. Kennedy are great examples of true leadership. Both fought for equal rights for all people and lost their lives doing so.

Former president Obama's chief of staff warned Obama to not consider universal health care, as he felt Obama would not get reelected for a second term. This warning did not bother former president Obama, as he was there to do the right thing. He was reelected, and universal health care did pass—even without the support of the Republican Party. This is courageous leadership: fighting bad press, ignorance, and opinions and **staying the course**. Former president Obama did have to compromise on some parts of the universal health care plan in order to get the necessary votes to pass it. Compromising is okay, as millions of people are now able to have health care.

Former president Obama's second courageous act as president was the assassination of Osama bin Laden—a global threat to all countries. Former president Obama had only three data points to use to decide if the compound that was targeted for the attack was bin Laden's home. The data points were so weak that if you approached a judge in the United States for a search warrant using these three data points, you would be denied. The three data points were: the targeted house had a six-foot wall, as compared to surrounding houses that had three-foot walls; this house burned trash, and other houses had trash disposed of differently; and there was no wiring going into the house like there was in the surrounding houses. That was the information given to former president Obama for him to use to decide whether this was bin Laden's home.

The administration did not even know if bin Laden would be present during the time of the raid. Former president Obama made a courageous decision based on limited information. His presidency would have taken a big hit if he were wrong. The raid was a success; no American lives were lost, and bin Laden was killed. (We did lose one of our two helicopters when it clipped the wall surrounding the house during the raid and had to be abandoned and destroyed. The occupants in the downed helicopter caught a ride in the remaining helicopter.) As a leader, the goal is not to get people to follow you; it is to **get people to join you**.

> *Doing something hard and doing the right thing are usually the same thing.*

Harriet Tubman

Harriet Tubman escaped from slavery in the South in the 1850s and, through a series of safe houses and routes, traveled to the North. She created the Underground Railroad process. She could have done what many people do today and say, "I got mine." She had her freedom and the ability to live a happy life. Instead, she kept crossing back into the

South and freeing slaves through the Underground Railroad. The slave masters had a bounty out for her, but they never caught her. Harriet Tubman freed hundreds of slaves and could have freed more, but she could not convince them that they were slaves. Why? These slaves were comfortable and conformed to their conditions.

This is the highest level of courageous leadership—in addition to that of Dr. Martin Luther King Jr.—that I can recall. She put her life on the line each time she crossed from South to North and North to South. She was driven to **help others** without even knowing them. Harriet Tubman is considered the Moses of the black community. Imagine you have your freedom after a life of slavery. Would you keep going back to help others, putting your life in danger each time?

You may be saying, "That is great, but how do I practice courageous leadership when there are many variables within my organization that limit me from being courageous?" There is a saying I want to share with you: if you do not stand for something, you will fall for anything. All leaders will have variables against them, but they need to **take a stand**, choose which initiatives to fight for, and practice courageous leadership. All leaders will have to compromise with stakeholders and let them have some victories. If all ideas and actions just come from you, then there is no need for a team. Compromising so others have victories is okay, as teammates need to have ownership and a stake in the team process.

Outside the Box

Vision

Where there is no vision, the people perish.

Proverbs 29:18 KJV

NBA legend Walt Frazier said, "Most people do not have the vision to see things that are different" (ESPN, 2017). I thought that statement was profound the first time I heard it. The fact that an NBA superstar of the 1970s understood vision was also impressive. Out-of-the-box visionary leadership is not only setting long-term organizational goals—it is also being able to analyze, evaluate, and create for your organization's benefit today. Meaning, **seeing things differently** now.

So what is vision? I remember many times in my teenage years and early twenties envisioning a better life for myself that consisted of living in a certain part of town, in a unique type of house, having a career where I was a respected leader leading an organization, and thinking of the hard work and long road to reach those goals. If you have had that type of thinking, those types of dreams, ideas, and endless thoughts about improving your present situation with the end result of a bright future, that is visionary thinking. Visionary **leaders are result oriented**.

> *We move toward what we consistently see.*
> *Keep your vision in front of you.*

Remember Dr. Martin Luther King Jr., who had a dream that all people would be treated equally? Recall former president John F. Kennedy's vision about reaching the moon? In his words, "We go to the moon not because it is easy but because it is hard." History points out that former president Abraham Lincoln fought to free slaves. All three visionary leaders mentioned gave their lives to move humanity forward. They gave momentum to great causes.

Visionary leaders are imaginative, visionary leaders can be pioneers, visionary leaders have the discipline to hold the end picture in mind. They are able to inspire teammates with their vision by tapping into emotions. They are bold and **do not accept failure** as an option. They are optimistic and see a setback as a setup for the future. They are collaborative and give their teammates flexibility to reach goals.

Visionary leaders have something they are extremely passionate about or deeply believe, and they articulate this vision to those around them to find like-minded people to fulfill the vision together. Great leaders with vision are people like Walt Disney, who envisioned Disneyland as a place where everyone could be happy. He sold this vision to a retired navy officer and won him over to the idea of being the chief man overseeing the construction of Disneyland (Michael, 2016).

Thomas Edison invented the lightbulb, yet teachers said he was too stupid to learn anything. He was fired from his first two jobs for being nonproductive. Edison made ten thousand unsuccessful attempts to invent the lightbulb before he succeeded. When a reporter asked, "How did it feel to fail ten thousand times?" Edison replied, "I did not fail ten thousand times. The lightbulb was an invention with ten thousand steps" (University of Kentucky).

The Apollo 13 mission in 1970 could have ended in tragedy, but due to visionary out-of-the-box thinking, three astronauts' lives were saved. The space module the astronauts were traveling in had an explosion that put them in a situation where it was possible they would not make it back to Earth. The NASA engineers on Earth had to figure out how to get the astronauts back.

A major concern was that the astronauts were quickly losing oxygen in the module. The engineers' approach was to gather all items that were in the module and place them on a large table in their office. Items placed on the table were clothes the astronauts were wearing, tools in the module, and all mission-related items inside the module. The engineers looked at all of the gathered items on the table and eventually figured out a method to keep the astronauts alive and get them back to Earth safely. It was a difficult task that took creative, visionary, out-of-the-box thinking.

You must endure the process to your vision
as it will bring you into your promise.
Bishop T. D. Jakes

Imagine standing on top of a mountain with a 360-degree view. You can see far and wide. Now, imagine walking on a crowded downtown sidewalk with many large buildings on both sides of the street. You have limited vision and can barely see five feet in front of you. Which view do you prefer?

In the same manner, it is best to organize your leadership role so that you have a 360-degree view of all areas. Never get stuck in the organizational mud of only knowing some details. You need to maximize your knowledge in order to make effective visionary decisions. **Organize your schedule** to allow yourself to have a true pulse on all departments.

Instinct

What is instinct? All of us are born with it, but only some people develop it. You cannot teach it. It is that gut feeling that occurs when something good or bad is about to happen. Your mind will tell you to answer a phone call when you typically do not answer calls that are listed as unknown. It is that feeling to do something you typically would not do; the feeling is very strong, so you do it. When sea turtles hatch on the beach, they have a choice to go inland or into the ocean. They go into the ocean. How do they know? It is their instinct.

Bishop T. D. Jakes published a book in 2014 called *Instinct* that I highly recommend. It discusses instinct within leadership. Many things in his book resonate with me, but his example of the giraffe and the tortoise stands out. Bishop Jakes explains how a giraffe eats from the top of trees and has far and wide vision. The giraffe can see if there is a raging fire to the east and knows not to head in that direction. The tortoise walks on the ground, eats from the ground, and has limited vision. The tortoise does not know that if it heads to the east, it will encounter a raging fire. Bishop Jakes adds that the tortoise will never understand the decision a giraffe makes because of its limited vision (Jakes 2014). Are you a giraffe or tortoise leader?

Bishop Jakes also mentions a trip to Africa when he was part of a guided safari tour to observe elephants. They were in a Jeep vehicle driving through the jungle, and it was one of the guides' jobs to look for elephants. This was difficult because of the dense jungle. As they were driving, the lookout yelled to the guide who was driving, "The elephant is over there." How did he know where the elephant was located when others could not see it? It was instinct, which the guide had developed over the years. Perhaps it was a smell, a sound, or damaged shrubs that triggered the lookout's instinct.

Leaders should constantly work on developing their instinct to assist with their leadership. This practice will save the leader many headaches and avoid unnecessary setbacks. I am convinced, from my observation of many leaders over the past thirty years, that what sets apart good leaders from great leaders is the instinct factor.

Humility

Humble Leadership

As I mentioned in the introduction, leadership is a defining moment and a blessing. Leadership should be taken very seriously. You have an opportunity to move a team to a synergy level and to **inspire individuals** to reach their potential. If you truly respect and embrace leadership, you should wake up each morning with excitement and a hungry for success attitude.

Too often I see people who receive an offer of employment to lead an organization celebrate, yet there is nothing to celebrate at that point—no body of work to rejoice over. Sure, it is okay to quickly pat yourself on the back because earning a leadership position is hard, but sustaining it is twice as hard. You never know if the team you are leading will sabotage you, if higher level leadership will turn on you, or if associates will never embrace you for whatever reason. Remember, you can lose your leadership position in an instant.

Treat people like you want to be treated, **be a role model leader,** find a balance of not being too flexible and not being too firm, and have a boldness of determination to make a difference. I was asked once, "Are you happy you are getting paid?" My response was, "Yes, but I also want to make a difference."

So what does *humility* mean? According to the dictionary, it is a modest or low view of one's own importance—humbleness. David Brooks, in his book *The Road to Character*, mentions a survey that was given to people in the 1950s and again in 2005. The same one question appeared on each survey: "Do you think you are important?" In the 1950s, 12 percent of those who responded checked yes. In 2005, 80 percent responded yes (Brooks 2016).

The 80 percent response rate does not surprise me due to the culture in today's world. We are all important in someone's eye. If you have kids, they see you as their example, your parents see you as their number one accomplishment, your spouse loves you and believes you are his or her shining star, and there are many other instances where people see you as an important figure in their lives.

We live in a world where the customer is always right and where some youth sports leagues don't keep score so there are no losers. A portion of today's parents are doing a questionable job with teachable moments and some kids are growing up expecting things to be handed to them.

Leaders and their teammates must understand that the team is more important than any individual. **Team movement** is more important than individual movement. There truly is no "I" in the word "team." I have read that the word "team" stands for "together everyone achieves more." Leaders must ensure team is their priority.

> *Humility does not mean you think less of*
> *yourself. It means you think of yourself less.*
> Ken Blanchard

Jim Collins published a book in 2001 called, *Good to Great.* It focuses on many effective leadership traits such as getting **the right people on the organizational bus** and the wrong people off the organizational bus, why an initiative can work for one organization but not succeed in another, and level-five leadership. Level-five leadership entails a leader who has professional will and humility. Collins mentions that organizations do not have to search for a nationally known superstar or a leader with a larger-than-life personality. His point is that leaders may not look the part, but if they have professional will and humility, they will succeed (Collins 2001).

When organizations hire, they should also focus on the humility factor during the interview process by reviewing a typical organizational situation that will occur and listen for a response that includes a humble solution. Reference checks are critical to ensure the candidate the organization is selecting to lead, truly does integrate humility into leadership practices. Leadership is not about the leader; it is about everyone else. What does the leader receive? The leader will receive attention, a nice salary, many fringe benefits, and the gratification of accomplishments.

Boss (Manager) versus Leader

Anyone can be a boss (manager). If you are reactive and love to point and shout, you will be a great boss that everyone dislikes. Bosses deal with the daily complexities within the organization and are not visionary people.

Leaders are visionary people with a focus on building partnerships with entities that can help their organization grow. Leaders look for additional funding sources to supplement inadequate funding to meet the organization's needs. Leaders research methods to operate efficiently within the organization. **Leaders have a 360-degree view** (sound familiar) of the organization. Leaders are not in-office leaders—one who stays in the office most of the time, they are out-of-office leaders—observing, listening, learning, and responding to needs, with **the goal of improving** their organization.

In his book, *On Becoming a Leader*, Warren Bennis states that leaders "master the context" rather than surrender to it. He makes the following distinctions between bosses (managers) and leaders:

- The manager administers; the leader innovates.
- The manager is a copy; the leader is an original.
- The manager focuses on systems and structures; the leader focuses on people.
- The manager relies on control; the leader inspires trust.
- The manager has a short-range view; the leader has a long-range perspective.

- The manager has his or her eye always on the bottom line; the leader has his or her eye on the horizon.
- The manager imitates; the leader originates.
- The manager is a classic good soldier; the leader is his or her own person.
- The manager does things right; the leader does the right thing (Bennis 2003).

When you hold any type of meeting, always sit with your team. Never sit to the side. Sitting to the side creates an us-versus-them environment.

The Leaders Edge: The Seven Keys to Leadership in a Turbulent World, by Burt Nanus, characterizes leadership as follows:

> Leaders take charge, make things happen, dream dreams, and then translate them into reality. Leaders attract the voluntary commitment of followers, energize them, and **transform organizations** into new entities with greater potential for survival, growth, and excellence. Effective leadership empowers an organization to maximize its contributions to the well-being of its members and the larger society of which it is a part. If managers are known for their skills in solving problems, then leaders are known for being masters in designing and building institutions; they are the architects of the organization's future (Nanus 1991).

I agree with both Bennis and Nanus. These leadership

characteristics are what we all should be aspiring to. However, I have observed many leaders over the years and have noticed a disturbing trend. Leaders should not utilize a cutthroat, political, or mean-spirited approach. There is no room for this abysmal leadership style. Manhandling a situation is a power tactic and is evidence of an insecure leader. An effective leader uses humanistic traits.

It is interesting how, during the interview process, candidates claim they are collaborative leaders, but when they start the job, they may often be the opposite. A leadership style that is not too flexible and not too firm (sound familiar) works best when working with teams.

Nipper

Culture

Leaders, never let your organizational culture get to a bad level. You want teammates helping each other not hurting one another. **Be a nipper!** A nipper is a leader who eliminates problems immediately.

Culture is the organization's expectations, behaviors, attitudes, beliefs, goals, principles, traditions, and practices. It is the social energy that drives (or fails to drive) organizations. **Culture is built up over time** as people work together, solve problems, and confront challenges. Think of culture as the soil of the organization. A fertile, healthy, rich soil can grow anything that is planted.

Leaders need to be aware of countercultures. Countercultures are groups of people that work against the overall mission and vision of the organization. These people work hard to interfere, damage, disrupt, harm, or sabotage the leader and his or her followers. Some countercultural people act covertly—with a smile, pretending they are true team members—while others act overtly—knowing how to cross the line and jump back at the right time in order to avoid getting fired.

Leaders that are nippers, put countercultural people in check to protect the organizational culture. To do this, you may need to have difficult conversations and written improvement plans. This may not be enjoyable, but great leadership includes being professionally tough (not mean) when you have to face difficult situations.

Once countercultural people are in check, do not ignore them, but do not spend a lot of time on them. Find that perfect balance. A mistake of a new or less-skilled leader is to spend 80 percent of their time on 20 percent of the employees, which are typically the countercultural people. A leader's energy and time should be focused on those teammates who are **committed to the mission and vision** of the organization: teaching them, praising them, rewarding them, and promoting them.

Progressive organizations address their culture first. As mentioned earlier, culture is the soil of the organization. Rich soil produces high expectations, intelligent behaviors, positive attitudes, strong beliefs, realistic goals, aligned principles, fun traditions, and smart practices.

Dr. Anthony Muhammad, in his 2012 State of Indiana speech called "Moving the Bus Forward: Creating Healthy Learning Environments for All Students," mentions a common mistake of many organizations. It is tempting to focus first on technical-structural items such as scheduling, the evaluation process, and professional development.

Consider, though, where culture is the soil, technical-structural is the seed. If an organization has bad soil, the seed will not bloom. This is why it is important to build your organizational culture first. As a leader you build organizational culture by meeting with your team face to face and doing the following:

- Listen to teammates through discussions, asking questions, and conducting surveys.
- Deliver the message of a need to change the current cultural state with a sense of urgency.
- Articulate how the **change will make the organization better**. Show the data. Present case studies.
- Create a new mission (why we exist).
- Develop a new vision (what we will become) with goals.
- Set a goal of meeting the needs of everyone (broad-based action) within your goals. This is a challenging task, but it can be done.
- Build in short-term goals as evidence of movement toward the long-term goals (Muhammad 2012).

You can use this methodology or a similar method. Ensure that you have a measurement tool to identify growth or regression within your method. A rubric is an effective measurement tool. You will discover many rubrics by conducting research. I prefer the Jim Collins rubric. It is simple but effective:

A = We exemplify our culture exceptionally well; there is limited room for improvement.

B = We often exemplify culture, but we also have room for improvement.

C = We show some evidence of our culture, but our record is spotty.

D = There is little evidence that we exemplify our culture, and we have obvious contradictions.

F = We operate almost entirely contrary to this trait (Collins 2006).

I recommend sitting down with your team on a quarterly basis to rate your team culture. You can use the Jim Collins rubric or another. Teams must be honest with themselves when rating their culture. After utilizing a rubric and finalizing a rating, organizations must create an improvement plan, as necessary fine-tuning must be a constant practice. This is what great organizations do.

Fear

Face fear with faith. When you are a leader, many people will doubt you, and at times you will doubt yourself. I repeat, **face fear with faith.** Voices inside your head will tell you that you are not ready, you don't belong in the room with other leaders, you are not smart enough, you are too young, you are too old, or you do not have the leadership talents this organization needs. You must talk over the negative thinking with words of faith. If you do not, the thinking will take over, and you will limit yourself by believing those negative thoughts.

Stay committed to your goals. There will be days you and your team will take ten steps forward, and there will be days your team takes fifteen steps back. Understand that this is part of the journey to reach your goals. Use the steps back as lessons learned and to sharpen your leadership skills. When you learn from your mistakes and do not make excuses for them, future steps back will be reduced to three or four instead of fifteen.

What you allow to play in your mind will determine what kind of leader you will be.

Frank Lloyd Wright once said, "I know the price of success: dedication, hard work, and an unremitting devotion to the things you want to see happen." Remember these things: the path to success is peppered with land mines; the pain of discipline is temporary; you will be hit with many punches, but do not get hit with the knockout punch; and **your destiny is always worth fighting for**.

Even though some people give you no respect, be intelligent when you put them in check. Because when you are ignorant, you get treated that way. Rapper Too Short, from his song, "The Ghetto."

Avoid being an easy, all right, but not nourishing leader. "On the road to destiny—halfway to the goal—every person will be tempted to give up. Some people turn around and go back; the others **stay committed** and keep moving forward. Both people travel the same distance, but one ends up at the starting line, and one goes forward to reach the goal. Committed people outlast the difficulty" (Osteen 2017).

In 1960, a young man—who was orphaned as a child—borrowed $900 and opened a pizza restaurant in Michigan.

He had a couple of bad breaks: first, his business partner broke into his account and stole his entire life savings, and then his restaurant burned to the ground in 1968. He could have given up, but he kept the faith. Shortly after the fire, he came up with an idea to take pizza to the people. Today, there are over six thousand Domino's Pizza establishments. Just recently, the founder sold his business for over $1 billion.

Shift your mind-set by not allowing your heart and mind to get stuck in the impossible. At times, we can get caught up in what we cannot do. The six inches between your ears and what is behind your rib cage are what make a difference. Face fear with faith.

Notes

Teach

Teach Everyone to Victory

If you want to lift yourself up, lift up someone else.
Booker T. Washington

One of Dr. Maya Angelou's quotes that I really appreciate is, "When you get, give. When you learn, teach." In leadership, **sharing expresses that you are not selfish**. If you have the magic formula for success, why not share it? In life, if people are genuine about helping one another, no person should be left behind—no matter where he or she lives, what color the person is, or how much money they have in the bank.

There have been many times in my career when I have observed leaders being selfish with great ideas and resources. We tend to forget that leadership—at any level—is not about the adults. It is about the mission (why the organization exist) and the vision (what the organization aspires to become). **Teach others, and help them grow.**

Be a mentor, a person who praises others, a volunteer, or a humble servant. Your talents are not to be kept in a jar or on a shelf. God gave us talents, skills, and knowledge to **make an imprint in the world**.

Organizations are complex because people are complex. It does not have to be this way. Be careful of having too much pride, selfishness, and the desire to be noticed. If someone treats you bad, **become better, not bitter**. Both actions use the same amount of energy, so why not choose the positive action. Believe that your actions become your legacy. Remember, we are a collection of our choices. Commit to believing in all team members by building goals that guide behaviors. Reflect by analyzing data and confronting those facts. Create a disciplined practice of collaboration to make adjustments as needed. Move from a *me* to a *we* leadership approach. Create an understanding with your team that one individual will only get us so far but the collective effort of the entire team will get the organization to the finish line.

In leadership, a recipe for disaster is poor preparation, a lack of support for team members, and task overload. If you are a new leader—or are aspiring to become a leader—shadow and observe strong leaders, surround yourself with smart people who have many perspectives, and ask yourself, **"What do I need to do to improve?"**

There are no classes called Gossip 101, Idiots 202, Mean Teammates 302, Resisters 415, Drama 523, and How to Be the Best Leader Ever 701. Teams will have people with various viewpoints, ideas, and philosophies. Ensure a professional practice of integrating these valuable thoughts.

Knowledge levels within your team will vary from no knowledge to very knowledgeable. **Provide support** to help grow the new or less skilled, and challenge and enhance teammates' capacities that are at a high level. Think of inspired methods to increase your teams' potential. You are going to need the best team you can build in order to achieve movement and success.

So, what do you teach leaders and followers on your team? You teach them to be **courageous**, smart, bold, different, unique, balanced, and exceptional; to make waves; to take a stand; and to be knowledgeable. Teach them to focus **outside the box** in the present and future. Teach them to have **humility**, as humble teams focus on supporting all associates. Teach them to **nip** bad cultures in order to progress forward. Teach them to educate themselves and then to **teach** others. Remember, leaders have something in them that causes others to stand out. Teaching is one of those components. Let's create future leaders!

> *You see things; and you say, "Why?" But I dream*
> *things that never were; and I say, "Why not?"*
> *George Bernard Shaw*

Review

Name two things that you learned in each section:

C = **C**ourage

_____

_____

O = **O**utside the Box

_____

_____

U = H**U**mility

_____

_____

N = **N**ipper

_____

_____

T = **T**each

_____

_____

References

30 for 30. "Survive and Advance—North Carolina State/ Coach Valvano Story." Originally aired March 17, 2013, on ESPNU.

Bennis, Warren. 2003. *On Becoming a Leader*. New York City: Basic Books.

Brooks, David. 2016. *The Road to Character*. New York City: Random House Publishing Group.

Collins, Jim. 2001. *Good to Great*. New York City: HarperCollins Publishers, Inc.

Collins, Jim. 2006. *Where Are You on Your Journey from Good to Great?* Jim Collins Rubrics. http://www. jimcollins.com/tools/diagnostic-tool.pdf.

Jakes, T. D. 2014. *Instinct*. New York City: FaithWords Hachette Book Group.

Michael. 2016. "Walt Disney. The New Leadership Model. Visionary Leadership." Accessed July 17, 2017. http:// www.leadershipgeeks.com/visionary-leadership/.

Muhammad, Anthony. 2012. "Moving the Bus Forward: Creating Healthy Learning Environments for ALL Students." YouTube video. Accessed March 3, 2017. https://www.youtube.com/watch?v=pj_qFBd4q38.

Nanus, Burt. 1991. *The Leader's Edge: The Seven Keys to Leadership in a Turbulent World.* New York City: McGraw-Hill.

Osteen, Joel. 2017. "Being Comfortable with Who You Are." Message delivered at Lakewood Church. Houston, Texas.

President Obama Story. 2017. "The 44th President: In His Own Words." Originally aired March 2017 on the History Channel.

University of Kentucky. 2017. "But They Did Not Give Up." Quotes compiled by the University of Kentucky. Accessed June 19, 2017. http://www.uky.edu/~eushe2/Pajares/OnFailingG.html.

About The Author

Dr. Anthony J. Perkins was born and raised in Connecticut. He presently resides in Buckeye, Arizona. He has served as an educational leader for almost three decades in the capacity of school teacher, vice-principal, principal, district director, and now school district superintendent. He holds a Master's Degree in Education with an emphasis in Diverse Learners and a Doctorate Degree in Educational Leadership. In addition to his school experience, Dr. Perkins is a part-time professor for Northern Arizona University and author of three additional books - Leadership: Wild, Wonderful, and Perfectly in Process, The Principle of Moments, and P3 - Purpose, Pride, and Progress. Dr. Perkins interests include physical fitness, golf, and jazz music. However, he enjoys spending most of his time with his beautiful daughter. Dr. Perkins can be reached at perkup67@yahoo.com.

Printed in the United States
By Bookmasters